INSIDE
VIDEO GAMES

BY MEG MARQUARDT

CONTENT CONSULTANT
David Culyba
Assistant Teaching Professor
Carnegie Mellon University

Core Library

An Imprint of Abdo Publishing
abdobooks.com

Cover image: Video games can allow players to have
immersive experiences in virtual worlds.

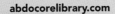

abdocorelibrary.com

Published by Abdo Publishing, a division of ABDO, PO Box 398166, Minneapolis, Minnesota 55439. Copyright © 2019 by Abdo Consulting Group, Inc. International copyrights reserved in all countries. No part of this book may be reproduced in any form without written permission from the publisher. Core Library™ is a trademark and logo of Abdo Publishing.

Printed in the United States of America, North Mankato, Minnesota
092018
012019

Cover Photo: Shutterstock Images
Interior Photos: Shutterstock Images, 1, 14, 24, 30, 40, 45; Mark Nazh/Shutterstock Images, 4–5, 43; The Picture Art Collection/Alamy, 7; Kevork Djansezian/Getty Images News/Getty Images, 9; Frederic J. Brown/AFP/Getty Images, 12–13; Klaus Balzano/Shutterstock Images, 19 (top); Gustoimages/Science Source, 19 (bottom); PR Image Factory/Shutterstock Images, 22–23; Ben Hoskins/FIFA/Getty Images, 29; Patrick T. Fallon/Bloomberg/Getty Images, 32–33; Wachirawit Iemlerkchai/Alamy, 37; Monkey Business Images/iStockphoto, 39 (top); iStockphoto, 39 (middle), 39 (bottom)

Editor: Megan Ellis
Series Designer: Ryan Gale

Library of Congress Control Number: 2018949761

Publisher's Cataloging-in-Publication Data

Names: Marquardt, Meg, author.
Title: Inside video games / by Meg Marquardt.
Description: Minneapolis, Minnesota : Abdo Publishing, 2019 | Series: Inside technology | Includes online resources and index.
Identifiers: ISBN 9781532117947 (lib. bdg.) | ISBN 9781641856195 (pbk) | ISBN 9781532170805 (ebook)
Subjects: LCSH: Technological innovations--Juvenile literature. | Video games--Juvenile literature. | Video games industry--Juvenile literature.
Classification: DDC 794.8--dc23

CONTENTS

GAMING MADE REAL

The player flies out into space. She is in charge of a top-of-the-line fighter ship. She is hunting down rebels. To complete her mission, she must find at least two enemy ships.

She flies the ship using the dashboard in front of her. It has many buttons and lights. Each button controls a different part of the ship. Some make the ship go up or down. Some make the ship go faster or slower. In front of her is a joystick with triggers. As soon as she finds her targets, she can use the joystick to shoot them down.

Virtual reality headsets block out the player's surroundings, making it feel like he or she is actually inside the game.

The player flies the ship around an asteroid field. She hears the rumble of the engines. If she accidentally steers the ship too close to an asteroid, she can hear the screech of metal as the ship crashes. Everything seems so real.

But it isn't real. The player is immersed in a virtual reality (VR) video game. In the real world, she has a VR helmet strapped to her head. She uses a controller to guide her ship as she plays the game. The VR helmet blocks out the rest of the world. The game feels like it is

Graphics in early video games such as *Spacewar* were extremely simple compared to today's games. Blocks and lines represented spaceships and lasers.

actually happening. The player is fully immersed in the game as a fearless fighter pilot.

An alarm sounds in the game. The radar on her ship has picked up an enemy. It's time to take care of the rebels.

THE ROAD HERE

The very first video game tournament was in 1972. The video game was *Spacewar*. Players attacked each other with spaceships. The graphics were not very good by today's standards. The spaceships looked like blocky triangles. There were no background graphics. It was just white ships on a black screen.

Video games have come a long way since *Spacewar*. As technology advances, the game industry creates cool new ways to play. In 1980, the computer game *Battlezone* was the first to use three-dimensional (3D) graphics. Those graphics were still blocky. Over the years, new consoles had more and more power. Game graphics improved and looked more realistic. By 2018, video games had advanced much further. They can look like animated movies brought to life. The graphics in video games such as *Mass Effect*, *Destiny*, and *The Legend of Zelda: Breath of the Wild* are jaw-dropping.

HARDWARE AND SOFTWARE

Advances in video game technology happen because of hardware and software. Hardware refers to the physical parts that make games possible, such as computers, gaming consoles, and mobile devices. It also includes parts such as controllers and screens. Graphics cards have become more advanced. They display information as images on a screen. New TVs can show games in

Games of the late 2010s such as *The Legend of Zelda: Breath of the Wild* have incredible levels of detail including grass that blows in the wind.

ultra high-definition (UHD). These TVs provide sharp images and dazzling colors.

Software is the set of instructions the computer or console follows. Designers, artists, and programmers all come together to create a game's software. Designers make maps and levels. Artists draw characters and scenery. Programmers make sure all the elements work together and use game engines to make it come to life. Software and hardware work together to make video games possible.

THE FIRST VIDEO GAME CONSOLE

Work on the first video game console began in 1966. Originally, it was a top-secret project. The US government wanted to use it to train soldiers. But many different people liked to play it. The console was called the Magnavox Odyssey. It was released in 1972. It did not plug into the wall. Instead, it used six small batteries. Most of the games were about sports. The graphics were simple. But the Magnavox Odyssey revolutionized video games. People could play in their homes instead of going to arcades.

THE FUTURE OF GAMING

Within the next few decades, video games may go through many changes. People won't just play on their phones or computers. With VR, they will jump into the game themselves. VR will make it feel like a game is completely real.

In order to make that happen, both software and hardware

need upgrades. Computer engineers, programmers, and game designers are creating a new wave of games. Video game technology continues to advance every year which creates more realistic and more interesting video games. Some of them may even be created by artificial intelligence (AI).

EXPLORE ONLINE

Chapter One talks about the history of video games. Since its start in the 1960s, the gaming industry has grown by leaps and bounds. Check out this source online that shows the history of gaming up to 2017. What are the most amazing advances not covered in this chapter? What are future games and technologies that you think would change how we play games?

VIDEO GAME HISTORY TIMELINE
abdocorelibrary.com/inside-video-games

COMPUTER AND CONSOLE HARDWARE

Gaming hardware covers a wide range of technology. Games can be played on many devices such as computers, gaming consoles, and phones. These devices are also called platforms. Each platform needs a different type of hardware. From controllers to mice, and chips to cards, hardware is where creating a great game starts.

CONSOLES AND COMPUTERS

There are many types of platforms. One way people play is on personal computers (PCs). To run cutting-edge games, PCs must

Gamers gathered at the 2018 Electronic Entertainment Expo (E3) to try out newly announced video games and consoles.

Players can add personal touches such as multicolored lights to PCs built from scratch.

be powerful. Complex graphics require a lot of computing power.

A gamer can build a gaming PC. Someone can buy all of the parts and put the PC together. Many people enjoy building gaming PCs. Some pre-built PCs don't have what the player needs. Building from scratch means the PC can exactly fit a gamer's needs.

Another way to play video games is on consoles. Consoles are types of computers designed for gaming. The player can plug them into a TV and start playing. Consoles have special controllers. Compared to a PC, they also make it easier for people to play together in the same room. New consoles are released every few years. In 2018, the most popular consoles were the PlayStation 4, Nintendo Switch, and Xbox One X.

INSIDE THE COMPUTER

Gaming systems can look pretty cool on the outside. They might have multicolored lights. Some might have cases covered in artwork from popular games. But the most important hardware is inside the computer or console.

As technology has advanced, video games have gotten better graphics. The game *Horizon: Zero Dawn* has some of the most detailed graphics. The main character wears furs and has feathers in her hair. The gamer can see every strand of fur and the fuzzy edges of the feathers. In order to show such detailed graphics, computers and consoles must be powerful. A high-definition (HD) or UHD TV isn't enough. One thing a computer needs is a graphics card. A graphics card is in charge of rendering the visual parts of a game. Rendering means taking computer code and turning it into an image. The better the graphics card, the more detailed the image.

Good graphics also need a good processor. The processor takes the instructions from a game and turns them into actions. It must process information quickly. A good processor stops a game from getting jumpy

ULTRA HD

TV technology has become better to support high-quality games. UHD is also called 4K HD because the TV screen is roughly 4,000 pixels wide. A 4K HD TV has approximately 8,300,000 pixels. A typical HD TV is roughly 2,000 pixels wide. It has approximately 2 million pixels. Each pixel displays one color. With four times as many pixels, a 4K TV can show very detailed images and video games.

or slow. The Xbox One X has one of the strongest processors. Processors are made up of cores. Cores are little instruction centers that process data. Consoles with more cores can more easily handle the information that a game creates.

STORAGE

Games can be stored in different ways. Some games are stored on discs. Computers and consoles access the game data using an optical drive. An optical drive uses a laser. It reads the data etched into the disc.

Many people also download games. The games are stored on a hard drive or memory chip. No separate disc is needed. The amount of space a game takes up is measured in bytes. The original *Legend of Zelda* game came out in 1986. It is 128 kilobytes (KB). *The Legend of Zelda: Breath of the Wild* came out in 2017. It is 13.4 gigabytes (GB). One GB equals 1 million KB. That means the latest Zelda game takes up more than 100,000 times as much space as the original one.

CONTROLLERS

Gamers can use controllers to make characters onscreen fight, jump, and explore. Some controllers have a directional pad, or D-pad. The D-pad is shaped like a cross. It has buttons for up, down, left, and right. It might move a character on the screen. It might also be used to choose options on a menu. Other buttons have letters or colors. These buttons can control actions, switch weapons, or perform other tasks.

Most controllers have more than just buttons. For example, the PlayStation 4 controller has two joysticks. They control character movement and camera angle. On the back of the controller are four buttons for firing weapons or doing special attacks. The PlayStation 4 controller also has a big touchpad at the top. The touchpad is for finger swipes and clicks.

Some controllers are designed for totally different gameplay. For example, the Nintendo Switch's main controller is called the Joy-Con. It can be split into

INSIDE A
CONTROLLER

Game controllers have many buttons. For example, the A button may cause a character to jump. The Xbox button turns on the console and controller. The left joystick can change a camera angle. When a player presses a button, this controls a circuit inside the controller. Look at the diagram below. Why might video game controllers have many circuits? How do these circuits work together to help someone play a game?

Left Bumper

Back Button

Xbox Button

Menu Button

X Button

Right Bumper

Y Button

B Button

Left Joystick

A Button

Directional Pad (D-pad)

Right Joystick

Circuits

Circuits

VIDEO GAME ACCESSIBILITY

Some disabilities make it hard for people to play video games. People who are blind or who have a hard time with the small buttons on controllers might not be able to play. Hardware engineers are working to bring games to everyone. They are designing controllers that can be used with only one hand or with a player's feet. Microsoft has the Xbox Adaptive Controller. The adaptive controller has two large buttons. But someone can program the buttons to do many different things. There are many ports on the back. Other devices such as joysticks and foot pedals can plug into the ports. A custom controller is one way to ensure that everyone can have fun playing video games.

two controllers. This makes it easy to play with friends. It also has an infrared sensor. Infrared sensors can sense objects in front of them. For example, the game *1-2-Switch* has a food-eating contest. The player holds the controller close to her mouth. As she pretends to eat food really fast, the controller can see when her mouth opens and closes.

STRAIGHT TO THE
SOURCE

Tara Voelker is the former chairperson of the International Game Developers Association group on video game accessibility. Voelker explains the importance of grading design students on accessibility:

> If they're graded on being colorblind-friendly for every project they have, they'll continue to think about it going forward. . . . In a lot of cases, accessibility isn't considered unless someone on the [development] team was [affected by] a disability that could impact the way they play a video game. . . . Over the years we've seen improvement on areas like subtitles and colorblindness, with even a handful of studios doing remappable controls. I'm also hearing more frequently about gamers with disabilities being part of playtesting or their feedback being reviewed and addressed.

> Source: Richard Moss. "Why Game Accessibility Matters," *Polygon*. Vox Media, August 6, 2014. Web. Accessed August 10, 2018.

What's the Big Idea?

Read the primary source text carefully. Then determine its main idea. Once you have the main idea, explain how it is supported by details. Name two or three of those supporting details.

SOFTWARE, CODING, AND DESIGN

Hardware works hand-in-hand with software. Software refers to the parts of a computer that aren't physically touchable. In other words, software is about computer code. Video game software includes art programs and gaming engines. As hardware advances, it lets software become more and more complex.

ART

Video game artists use powerful software. They might start by sketching out a character on paper. Then they make a basic 3D model of

Programmers use computer code to create software. They can then test this code to make sure a game works correctly.

3ds Max lets artists create detailed characters and
environments in 3D.

the character. Common programs are Maya, 3ds Max,
and ZBrush. These programs allow artists to look at
models from every angle. Users can rotate the models
and see the models in action.

Artists use software to make detailed characters.
They add textures and lighting effects to make
characters look realistic. They add animations to
create facial expressions or complicated movements.

Artists make sure characters look natural when they pick up objects or interact with the game world.

PROGRAMMING

Programmers write computer code. This computer code brings games to life. Programmers help characters move, talk, and interact with the game world. They program many different things. Some programmers create the physics of the world. Physics refers to how characters and objects move through the world. For example, programmers have to make code for how gravity works. If a character throws a ball, programmers

CODING GAMES

People who work with gaming software often know how to code. Because coding is so important, some websites have turned coding into a game. Websites such as code.org and CodeCombat teach the basics of how code works. Players learn how to program for given scenarios. They also learn how to make characters move and fight. All the while, they are learning how to code. These sorts of games may be training the next generation of game designers.

decide how many times it bounces. They also decide what that bounce sounds like and whether the ball hurts the character if it bounces against her. One way to do this is with conditional statements. Conditional statements are also known as "if-then" codes. For example, if a ball hits a character going very quickly, then it's going to hurt that character.

Conditional statements can be complicated. For example, some games have fighting. They use combat systems to create rules for the fights. A programmer writes code to say how much damage a punch does when it hits a character. But not all hits in

TWINE

Some games do not have fancy, expensive graphics. They are based only in words and a few images. Twine is a software tool that lets users make text-based games. These games are also called Interactive Fiction. Twine games tell stories. A designer makes a vast, sprawling world of text. A player picks the character's next moves. Depending on what the player chooses, the game presents different possibilities.

the game are equal. A hit from far away doesn't do as much damage. This type of coding makes the game feel more realistic.

ARTIFICIAL INTELLIGENCE

AI impacts every aspect of a game. While the player makes choices for their character, all the other characters in the game react. These other characters are called non-player characters (NPCs).

Advances in AI mean smarter NPCs and more fun gameplay. For example, in *Star Wars*: *The Old Republic*, an NPC companion follows the player around. That companion can heal the player to keep his character alive. AI controls that character. If the player's health drops below a certain level, the NPC knows to send out a blast of healing power. AI keeps the character alive.

In a basketball game, AI opponents decide when to shoot the ball or pass to a teammate. In a shooting game, AI enemies take cover and try to surround the character. In a chess game, the AI tries to think several moves ahead to outsmart the player.

AI is also responsible for building the world around the player. The game *Skyrim* is full of endless possibilities because of AI. People wrote a storyline for the game. This includes quests and checkpoints. But based on the player's level and location in the game, AI also generates random quests. *Skyrim* is a type of game called an open-world game. Some games have a strict order that the player has to follow. But in an open-world game, a character can wander all over the map. They can discover new things to do or even new places to visit.

GAME ENGINES

Art, programming, and AI come together in the game engine. A game engine is the programming behind a whole game. Many different games can use the

AI controls other players on a sports team such as those in *FIFA 18*. The AI teammates must know how to make decisions based on what's happening in the game.

Fortnite is available on many consoles, including the Nintendo Switch.

same engine. A game engine helps keep some types of code the same. For example, an engine can provide the code to simulate gravity. Then gravity works the same throughout all of the games that use the engine. Programmers do not need to write the code every single time. Other things in the game engine could include how animations work, how audio is played, and how the graphics are rendered.

One of the most popular game engines is called Unreal. It is used by many different game companies for games such as *PlayerUnknown's Battlegrounds*, *Fortnite*, and *We Happy Few*. Though each game company can make changes and tweaks to the engine, Unreal is a starting point. This allows the companies to focus their effort into creating more detailed artwork and storylines.

MAKING SMARTER COMPUTERS

Chapter Three talks about advances in AI. What evidence can you find to support this point? Go to the website below. Does the information on the website support the main point of the chapter? What other points does the source bring up about AI?

WHAT IS ARTIFICIAL INTELLIGENCE?
abdocorelibrary.com/inside-video-games

THE FUTURE OF VIDEO GAMES

Video game technology gets more advanced every year. As AI becomes stronger, computers may design games themselves. Augmented reality (AR), VR, and game streaming will change the way players interact with games.

AI-DESIGNED GAMES

AI is used for creating realistic enemies and companions. It might also generate random quests or monsters to fight. But in the future, AI might create brand-new games.

Some AI programs can design entire levels of video games. Programmers take hundreds of levels from previous games. The AI then analyzes the data from the levels. It creates new levels based on that analysis. It sees patterns in the levels. AI might even make levels that are more challenging and more unexpected than a level made by humans.

In the future, AI might also write a story based on information given by a programmer. It may create rules and combat systems for the game. Eventually, AI may be able to build a whole video game from scratch.

MOTION CAPTURE

One way to make more realistic games is to use motion capture. Motion capture uses real actors. The actors are covered in sensors. Cameras and computers capture the actors as they move around a stage. The actors may be acting out scenes. They might be throwing punches or shooting arrows. These actors' movements are then animated by artists and programmers. Motion capture has been especially good for realistic facial expressions. If a character in a game looks real when she is speaking, there's a good chance a real actor played out the character's scenes.

AUGMENTED REALITY AND VIRTUAL REALITY

Game designers are planning games that put the player in the middle of the action. Players won't watch the action on a screen. Instead, they'll feel like they are in the video game world.

AR brings the game into the real world. On smartphones, AR puts game elements over images from a camera. On other devices such as the Microsoft HoloLens, the game elements are layered over the user's view of the real world. Mobile games drive AR technology. One popular AR game is *Pokémon Go*. In *Pokémon Go*, players walk around to catch fun creatures. The game uses the camera in a phone or tablet. It puts a 3D model of the creature on the ground in front of the player. The player then swipes the screen to catch or battle the Pokémon. AR makes the real world seem more fantastic.

VR may also be the future of video game technology. In VR, the player actually steps into a whole new world. In a soccer game, the player might have to run and kick right along with her teammates. New technology might even let the players smell fresh-cut grass as they play. VR has the potential to be fully immersive.

GAME STREAMING

Streaming is when a player views or uses content that is stored somewhere else. For example, Netflix is an app for streaming movies and TV shows. Twitch is an app for streaming videos of other people playing

CAPTURING EMOTIONS

Though VR is all about capturing the senses right now, there's another way it might advance gaming. Developers are also interested in capturing emotion. Imagine talking to a player who is happy but has a blank facial expression. Something would seem off.

A new wave of VR technology is being built to read how a player's face is changing. It will be able to tell if a player is smiling or frowning. Then the player's character in-game will change, too.

Ingress was one of the first AR games. Players walk around and capture portals that are located in the real world.

video games. But some people want to stream entire games to their computers so they can play them.

As of 2018, users can download games onto platforms. With streaming, the game would be stored in a data center far away. Players would connect to the internet. The game would stream right onto their TV. In June 2018, Netflix announced a version of *Minecraft* that could be streamed through Netflix. It is called *Minecraft Story Mode*. The player would use a TV remote to control the character.

Programmers and hardware engineers have to make gameplay faster before streaming is more common. Players do not want to wait for characters to move or do an action. Once video games can be streamed, more people can play them. A player would not need an expensive computer or gaming console, but they would need an internet connection.

With more people playing, that means more chances for fun new games. As technology advances,

VIDEO GAME
STREAMING

Video game streaming would allow people to play games that are stored far away. They would not have to buy expensive hardware. But many pieces of hardware work together to make game streaming possible. Take a look at the diagram below. How might game streaming help people access more video games?

4 **1**

3 **2**

1. Users press buttons while playing a streaming game. These button presses are transmitted through the internet.

2. The video game is running on a computer at a data center. It receives the data from the buttons.

3. The computer sends streaming video of the game back to the users.

4. The users react to what happens in the streaming game footage and press more buttons.

Minecraft Story Mode is available for consoles such as the Nintendo Switch. But streaming would make the game available to people who do not have consoles.

so will games. Before long, playing a video game will be like stepping into a movie or another world entirely. No matter what direction it goes, the future of gaming is bright.

STRAIGHT TO THE
SOURCE

Yves Guillemot founded Ubisoft, a video game company that makes AAA games. AAA games are big-budget games such as *Call of Duty* and *Destiny*. Guillemot believes game streaming is the next big thing for AAA games. In an interview with *Variety*, Guillemot discussed the future of game streaming:

> It is going to help the AAA game industry grow much faster. We have to work on the accessibility of those games, to make sure they can be played on any device, but the fact that we will be able to stream those games on mobile phones and television screens without a console is going to change a lot of the industry. . . . Eventually, the technology will improve dramatically, which will allow us to have a very smooth experience in the big cities of the world.

Source: Brian Crecente. "Ubisoft Believes Next Gen Is the Last for Consoles." *Variety*. Variety, June 6, 2018. Web. Accessed July 31, 2018.

Back It Up

Guillemot is using evidence to support a point. Write a paragraph describing the point the author is making. Then write down two or three pieces of evidence the author uses to make the point.

FAST FACTS

- Video game technology includes hardware and software.

- New hardware allows game designers to make more detailed games. The games may have bigger worlds, better graphics, or more characters.

- Many games use controllers with buttons and joysticks. Other new controllers such as Nintendo's Joy-Con provide new options for interacting with games.

- New software allows games to be more realistic. Artificial intelligence creates realistic enemies as well as companions that help a player on a mission. In the future, AI may even design entire levels or games.

- Programmers use code to control elements such as character movements, reactions, and interactions. Some code creates game physics, which control elements of the world such as gravity and motion.

- Augmented reality games use a camera on a smartphone or tablet to put video game elements into the real world.

- Virtual reality games use a headset to make the player feel as though he or she is in a virtual world.

STOP AND
THINK

Tell the Tale

Chapter Three talks about how important artists are to video games. Imagine you are an artist for a video game studio. Write 200 words about the sort of creatures you would create for your video game. What would these creatures be good at? Be sure to include many details.

Surprise Me

Chapter Four discusses the future of video games. After reading this book, what two or three facts about the future of gaming technology did you find most surprising? Write a few sentences about each fact. Why did you find each fact surprising?

Say What?

Studying video games and technology can mean learning a lot of new vocabulary. Find five words in this book you've never heard before. Use a dictionary to find out what they mean. Then write the meanings in your own words and use each word in a new sentence.

Take a Stand

Video game streaming is great for places with fast internet, such as big cities. However, they may not be great for people without fast internet. Look back through the book. Are there other places where game technology might not be available for everyone? How would you help game designers and programmers create games available for everyone?

GLOSSARY

arcades
places where people can go to play video games

artificial intelligence (AI)
a machine that simulates human thoughts and behaviors

game industry
the economy around creating, selling, and playing video games

graphics
visuals on a screen, such as a TV or a computer monitor

infrared
light rays that any warm object emits

joystick
a stick used to control movement in a game

pixel
a tiny area on a screen that displays a small part of graphics; a screen is made up of many pixels

three-dimensional (3D)
having the three dimensions of length, width, and height

touchpad
a small panel that is sensitive to touch

ONLINE RESOURCES

To learn more about video games, visit our free resource websites below.

Visit **abdocorelibrary.com** for free Common Core resources for teachers and students, including vetted activities, multimedia, and booklinks, for deeper subject comprehension.

Visit **abdobooklinks.com** for free additional online weblinks for further learning. These links are routinely monitored and updated to provide the most current information available.

LEARN MORE

Smibert, Angie. *Inside Computers*. Minneapolis, MN: Abdo, 2019

Woodcock, John. *Coding Games in Scratch*. New York: DK Publishing, 2016.

INDEX

About the Author

Meg Marquardt has been gaming since she was a little girl. Today, she loves to research and write about game design, E-Sport competitions, and more. She lives in Madison, Wisconsin, with her two scientist cats, Lagrange and Doppler.